Smart RV k

Your cookbook for
easy, delicious & healthy
camper meals

Carolin Uhrich

Notes

Contents

Comments on this Cookbook

<< Why this cookbook wanted to be written >>

This is how the cookbook came to life

My husband, my little son and I live in Germany. A few months after he was born, we went on our first motorhome holiday together in Portugal in 2017. By then, it was clear that we would buy our own. Many short and a few longer camper trips in Germany and Europe followed. We enjoy the freedom that camping brings.

Fresh and delicious camper food is important to us on the go. We notice that eating healthy and staying in nature is good for us. Breakfast planning is easy. We eat cereal or sandwiches and sometimes scrambled eggs. When we are on campsites, we occasionally use the food service. In between we snack on fruit, raw vegetables, yogurt, cheese cubes, boiled eggs, nuts and so on. We are also a well-rehearsed team when it comes to grilling. But when preparing warm meals and salads in the RV kitchen, new challenges kept cropping up.

The search for easy, delicious and healthy camping recipes was often neglected during travel preparations. Accordingly, we had one or two surprises. I triggered the smoke alarm with fried bacon. We often had to guess the quantities of ingredients without kitchen scales or, for example, we couldn't pour quinoa because our sieve was too coarse. In our little 6-meter vehicle we don't have an oven, a hand blender or a dishwasher. Our work surface is small. But that's fine. The main thing is that the RV kitchen is tidy, equipped with useful things, and we can look at our travel destination through the kitchen window while cooking in the motorhome.

With high-quality ingredients in the cupboards and delicious recipes at hand, we can fill our hungry stomachs around the clock. When out and about in nature, we often have few opportunities to make bulk purchases. That's why we buy most of it at home. Fresh ingredients and regional specialties are bought on the way. In between, we also go to restaurants and cafés.

Good preparation helps us enormously. The internet is not always available for research and cooking instructions at parking spaces in nature. So I started collecting suitable camping recipes that we tried out and optimized. On the way, we write the planned camping dishes on a piece of paper to keep track of which meals are planned and cross out the prepared meals.

Our preferences vary depending on the weather. In the cold season we like cooked food. In warm weather, we eat more salads and snacks. Basically, we try to cook in the motorhome with ingredients that smell somewhat subtle. Fat steam, which is produced when searing steak and fish in the pan, can build up in the textiles without an extractor fan. Cooking on hot days can add extra heat to a motorhome or camper van. On these days, preparation outdoors, e.g. on a grill with a hotplate, is a good idea.

The more extensive the recipe collection became, the more it occurred to me to share our cooking experiences with motorhome and van fans. I hope that the easy, delicious and healthy camping recipes will also meet your taste. If so, then I would really appreciate a review on Amazon. If you have any suggestions or questions, please email me: "carolin.uhrich@gmail.com".

That's why the cookbook has no pictures

You will probably be surprised that there are no pictures in this camping cookbook. There are several reasons for this:

1. I can cook better than take photos.
2. Most of the time, the food is eaten up before I can take a picture.
3. The camping dishes in this cookbook are very easy to prepare.

Therefore, I hope for your understanding and your creativity. Fortunately, in my experience, this is one of the core competencies of campers.

The camping recipes are measured for 2 people

I have two very different eaters by my side. My husband usually has a big appetite and is open to new recipes. My little son has his very own idea of food. He prefers to eat smaller amounts more often and is suspicious of new things. Therefore, the recipes in the cookbook are designed for 2 people and are usually generous. So my husband gets full, and our little darling can eat with us if he wants.

Why we want to cook healthy on the go

When on holiday, culinary temptations await at every piazza and at every mountain hut. However, ice cream and sweet cut-up pancake with raisins in large quantities have unpleasant side effects. So that we can fit into our favorite clothes even after the holiday, many of our camping recipes are an antithesis. Have we already eaten a lot of meat today? Then the next thing we do is cook a vegetarian or vegan recipe. Have we devoured a mountain of carbohydrates in the form of bread, pasta or pizza? Then we cook low-carb to compensate. And vice versa. The main thing is that healthy and tasty are not mutually exclusive. We like variety in camping food.

Basically, we prefer to eat as few finished products as possible. This avoids unnecessarily high amounts of sugar, problematic preservatives and harmful trans fatty acids. Still, there is no camping holiday without our little vices: chocolate for me and chips for my husband.

Life Hacks for Preparation

<< Useful knowledge for the kitchen crew >>

This is how motorhome & vanlife fans make their life easier

1. Plan thoroughly

We usually plan our meals for around a week. We leave "gaps" when we know we are going to eat out. The camping recipes with fresh ingredients come first, then the recipes with frozen ingredients, and finally the recipes made from durable ingredients. When supplies run out, planning and shopping are done again. On longer vacations, we take more of the durable ingredients with us. Planning takes time in advance, but it pays off on vacation.

2. Buying the right amount of food

If possible, we base our recipes on whole cans, jars or packaging. When a lot of opened ingredients pile up, it becomes too confusing for us. It is easier for us if we weigh and buy the used amount of vegetables in the supermarket in advance.

3. Hygienic storage of meat and fish

We prefer to buy the required quantity of meat from the butcher. We have it vacuumed for the holidays, then it stays fresh longer. For chunks of meat, we let the butcher cut the meat into small pieces. We freeze it if we don't already know when to make the dish. We always have minced meat in stock in the form of flat, frozen, vacuum-sealed plates. It can be thawed in warm water within a few minutes.

4. Protect your hands

When cutting chili, pumpkin, zucchini and beetroot, it is best to wear black disposable gloves. This prevents the hands from being stained by beetroot. It reduces the chances of getting chili in the eye and prevents dry hands from the stubborn vegetable juice of pumpkin or zucchini. The gloves can be washed off and used a couple of times.

5. Direct loading

We put the refrigerator in our motorhome into operation one day or a few hours before the trip. Then we buy the groceries for the trip. After shopping, the ingredients are loaded directly into the motorhome. Shortly before departure, the rest of the food comes from the kitchen at home.

6. Saving dishes

I especially love one-pot dishes because they taste great and save time washing up. For example, curries are incredibly delicious. We often eat them without rice. On the one hand to reduce carbohydrates and on the other hand because we can then eat more of them. Two birds with one stone!

7. Prepare Ingredients

At the beginning of cooking, we lay out the required ingredients. In the motorhome we have the bed as a shelf next to the kitchen. After laying out, we know that everything is in stock and do not have to open cupboards multiple times. If something is left lying around in the end, we know what still needs to be prepared.

8. Ventilate well

If you cook with gas, you should ensure that there is a slight draft when cooking in the mobile home or van. The more windows and doors that are opened while cooking, the fewer odors there are in the vehicle. Placing the lid on the pot also helps.

9. Rinse off immediately

While cooking, we directly wash the utensils used. Immediately after dinner, one of us washes up the rest of the motorhome. As long as the food on the dishes is still damp, it almost works by itself. We find scrubbing off dried-up food annoying. Ideally, we also dry off straight away, clear everything up and be ready to start again.

10. Remodeling and organizing

If you don't have enough space in the refrigerator and aren't taking anything frozen with you, you can remove the freezer compartment. It is also worth installing suitable baskets, boxes and organizers if it is your own vehicle. This will reduce the sliding, rattling and searching for your things. We have the following rule: "Everything has its own place"

Helpful utensils in the galley

The needs of different motorhome and van households are very different. Our wish is on the one hand to travel minimalistic and on the other hand to prepare lots of fresh dishes. Since we rarely bake at home, we never miss an oven on the way. After several trips, the following equipment has become established in our camper kitchen:

1. **Tableware**

   4 knives
   4 forks
   4 tablespoons
   4 teaspoons
   6 flat plates
   3 large bowls
   2 small bowls
   2 small glasses made of plastic
   2 cups
   2 wine glasses in a foam cube
   2 drinking bottles for driving and excursions

2. **Cookware**

   1 large bread knife
   1 large smooth knife
   1 small smooth knife
   1 coated pan with lid

3 pots with lids that fit into each other
2 trivets made of cork
1 wooden spoon
1 wooden ladle
1 wooden spatula

3. Kitchen Gadgets

1 measuring cups
1 handpresso pump and espresso pods
1 manual multi-chopper (900 ml)
1 spice box with index
1 grinder for salt and pepper (2 in 1)
1 scissors
1 measuring cup with different scales
1 foldable plastic sieve
1 foldable plastic sink (for the campsite)
1 small cutting board with juice groove
1 small whisk (to whisk salad sauce in the glass)
1 metal grater for cheese and vegetables with collecting basket
1 lemon squeezer
1 Vegetable peeler
1 potato fork
1 bottle opener
1 corkscrew
1 wine disc
1 wine closure
1 lighter
3 pairs of disposable gloves
1 ice cube mold

4. Rinsing & Cleaning

1 dish sponge
1 dishcloth
1 washing-up liquid (transferred to a small bottle)
1 drainage strainer
2 tea towels
1 roll of paper towels

1 box cosmetic tissues
1 bottle of all-purpose cleaner
1 hand soap
1 hand towel

5. Maintaining Order

1 big box for storing empty lunch boxes and snack boxes
1 box for glasses, cups and tea bags
1 box for storing fresh bread and corn waffles
1–2 boxes for storing fruit and vegetables (depending on the duration of the trip)
1 box for snacks
Felt inlays between dishes and pots (to prevent rattling)
Freezer bags for leftovers
system for residual waste, plastic, paper and glass
garbage bags
shopping bags
sealing clips, foldback clips and rubber rings
Bottle bag for storing vinegar, oil, muesli, nuts, pasta, rice, etc.
Storage for durable ingredients

6. Individual stuff

Depending on requirements, every camping household adds additional dishes for children and pets. If you like to bake or make casseroles on the go, you can take a camping oven for the gas stove with you.

We do without tablecloths, place mats, candles and napkins - but if you value them, you should treat yourself to it.

Our favorite ingredients

When it comes to ingredients, we usually focus on one all-rounder per category in order to save space. These are our preferences and experiences:

1. Cauliflower rice / Broccoli rice

Cauliflower rice is not rice, but cauliflower that has been chopped to the size of a grain of rice. For example, in a multi-shredder. It is mild in taste, low-carb, low in calories and can be prepared very quickly. It is conveniently offered frozen in the supermarket. So it's a wonderful alternative to traditional rice. Broccoli rice is the same in green. Here, the soft part of the broccoli stalk was chopped up to the size of a grain of rice.

2. Bread

We buy sprouted bread from the organic supermarket. It is bread made from sprouted grains. It is particularly digestible and stays fresh for days. Furthermore, it can be frozen well and thawed again overnight. If it is coated with butter and then topped with egg, avocado, sausage or cheese, it will fill you up. Topped with smoked salmon and coated with grainy mustard or horseradish, it is also very tasty.

3. Stock / Broth

Stock in the form of powder is the most practical. Nevertheless, we indulge ourselves in luxury and, depending on the recipe, take poultry or beef stock in liquid form with us. We love the taste and believe in the health benefits. For vegetable stock and also for seasoning sauces, I prepare a vegetable stock paste before the trip. The fresh vegetable stock paste can be kept in the refrigerator for weeks.

4. Vinegar

Our all-rounder for vinegar is white balsamic vinegar.

5. Shrimps

We mostly buy frozen shrimps from organic aquaculture. Without a shell and pre-cooked. Less effort and very durable. Before cooking, the protective glaze must be thawed, otherwise the food will be watered down. To thaw, we put the shrimp in the plastic packaging in lukewarm water and rinse them off at the end. If it has to be done very quickly, we rinse it directly in a sieve with warm water until the protective glaze is removed.

6. Minced Poultry

Poultry meat is lower in fat than beef or pork. In addition, it has a milder taste, which is especially good with children. We buy it frozen in the organic supermarket.

7. Honey

Liquid honey with a mild taste, such as blossom honey, is ideal for cooking and for salads. Traveling in France, we discovered our love for lavender honey.

8. Ginger

We love fresh ginger. If you prefer, you can also use ginger powder. If you cook with ginger frequently, you can prepare a long-lasting ginger paste to save time.

9. Coconut Milk

Creamy coconut milk with 90% coconut extract tastes particularly good and is not watery.

10. Herbs

We have some herbs like basil at home. In wintertime in hydroponic pots in the kitchen and in summer in our small garden. Before traveling, we cut some stems off, put them in a box with wet tissues and store them in the refrigerator. Our herbs usually stay fresh up to one week. Bought cress or microgreens are also very good to take away. If it has to go quickly while cooking, we cut the herbs over the food with kitchen scissors.

11. Canned Ingredients

We buy diced tomatoes, beans, chickpeas and corn in a jar or in a can. We prefer glasses because we can see what's inside right away. Furthermore, we think it is important that no sugar is added to our canned ingredients. This can be the case with kidney beans and chickpeas. The vegetables should be so tasty that they taste good straight out of the jar. The only way to do this is to try it out - there are big differences in taste between different brands.

12. Garlic

We usually buy garlic as a bulb and cut the cloves on site. Sometimes, we put pieces of garlic in oil at home. Garlic powder can also be a practical alternative.

13. Leek

We use the white and light green part of the leek. In some dishes, half of the leek is left over. In this case, the leek can be used in another dish instead of an onion. This is also a real insider tip for anyone who bothers crying while chopping onions. Leek is steamed briefly and should not brown, otherwise it can become bitter.

14. Oil

We use olive oil for almost everything. We buy extra virgin olive oil with a mild taste (not naturally cloudy so that it can be heated). The oil is stored in the motorhome from spring to autumn. If the temperature in the RV is low in wintertime, olive oil gets solid. Very fresh olive oil straight from the producer can have some spiciness, which I personally don't like. For Asian dishes, we pack small bottles of peanut oil, light sesame oil or ghee as required.

15. Pasta

Fusilli is a type of pasta that can really do everything. Due to their shape, they absorb the sauce well, cook quickly and are easy for children to eat. For one-pot dishes, we only use fusilli made from durum wheat semolina. Spelled or legume noodles get too mushy. If the sauce is cooked separately, spelt noodles are popular with us because they cook faster and seem to be even more digestible.

16. Black Pepper

We prefer black pepper made from freshly ground black peppercorns. It is easy to dose and adjust the grinding degree. The grinders are usually designed for this kind of pepper. Colored pepper often contains berries that are not tolerated by all mills.

17. Pine Nuts / Cedar Nuts

Roasted pine nuts are a poem, but nowadays, they are so expensive in the supermarket that I am speechless. That is why I order 500 g cedar kernels online if required. Visually, the two types of kernels hardly differ and in terms of taste I find cedar kernels almost even better than pine nuts. When roasting, you have to keep an eye on the kernels and stir occasionally. As soon as they are browning, roasting must be stopped, otherwise they will turn black and inedible.

18. Rice

White parboiled long grain rice cooks quickly, does not get mushy, and tastes good with everything.

19. Red Curry Paste

Our all-rounder for Asian cuisine. If you like the yellow or green paste better, you can of course use this instead.

20. Salt

We buy rock salt in a 500 g pack and refill it. Rock salt is fossil sea salt and contains some iodine. In addition, we plan to eat sea fish once or twice a week to get enough iodine.

21. Mustard

Medium-hot mustard spices up salad dressings and gives them a creamy consistency. The sugar in the mustard adds a slight sweetness to the sauce.

22. Soft Tomatoes

Soft tomatoes are more practical to process than fresh tomatoes or tomatoes in oil.

They are sun-dried tomatoes that have been softened in a hot water bath and will keep for a very long time in the closed packaging.

23. Soy Sauce

My husband loves the very classic soy sauce. I like the milder Tamari soy sauce for sushi. But we use the classic soy sauce for cooking.

24. Sweeteners

Some dishes need a little sweetness for a balanced taste. We use table sugar, honey or maple syrup, depending on the recipe. I don't use agave syrup because it contains too much fructose in my opinion. Honey in particular is practical because it is on board for breakfast anyway.

25. Tomato Paste

My favorite is double concentrated tomato paste, as it binds well and makes the food slightly sweet.

26. Lemons & Lime

Citrus fruits give many Asian recipes a great flavor. Even if only ½ lemon or lime is used, I squeeze one whole and drink the rest as a shot. Sour makes fun and hopefully the immune system is strengthened. My son likes to drink lemon juice diluted with cold water. In warm dishes, we add the lemon juice at the very end so that the vitamin C is largely retained.

27. Onions

We use small yellow onions for the dishes. When chopping onions and garlic, I make sure to use the "general purpose" side of the cutting board. The other side is reserved for fruit so that the taste of the onions does not carry over.

We always have this food on board

Our motorhome is our second household. We want to carry as little as possible back and forth before departure. At the same time, we don't want to drive around unnecessary things. That is why we only have a few selected basic ingredients on board and load the other ingredients for the planned meal before each trip.

We have a 2 in 1 **salt & pepper mill**. We also keep a **nutmeg** in a nutmeg grater. We use several compatible spice boxes at home and in the mobile home. These are small, labeled plastic boxes in a magazine file. Two spice cards with 6 compartments each are always on board and contain the following:

> **salt** coarse-grained (to refill the salt mill and for pasta water)
> **black pepper corns** (to refill the pepper mill)
> **sugar** fine-grained
> **sweet pepper powder**
> **oregano** (alternative: spice mixture "Italian herbs")
> **thyme**
> **chili powder**
> **curry powder**
> **turmeric powder**
> **cumin**
> **garam masala** (spice mixture)
> **ras el-hanout** (spice mixture)

In Summer, we have **vinegar** and **olive oil** on board in a bottle bag. In winter, however, we temporarily take out the two bottles. The olive oil solidifies in the bottle between about 4 and 10 degrees. It does not harm the quality, but the olive oil can only be used again if it has been warmed up in front of a heater outlet, for example. Vinegar freezes at just over 0 degrees, which can cause the bottle to burst.

Many ingredients for breakfast and main meals do not have to be refrigerated and can therefore be easily stored on board:

UHT-milk
oat flakes, muesli, corn flakes
honey
tea bags, coffee pods (individually packed)
corn waffles, crispbread or similar
pasta, soup noodles
rice
red lentils
pine nuts/cedar nuts, sunflower seeds and **walnuts**

Food in jars, canned food and cardboard boxes also last a long time. The disadvantage is their higher weight. Of the canned goods listed below, we therefore only store those products on board that are difficult to get on the go or where we have focused on our favorite products:

passed or cooked diced tomatoes
tomato paste
coconut milk
corn
various beans
chickpeas
tuna and mackerel in a can

As an emergency reserve, we always have a six-pack with 1.5 l water bottles and some canned food in the rear garage, which are not used.

The kitchen checklist for departure

Experience has shown that the last hours and minutes before departure are turbulent. Especially when children are bustling around you, it can be difficult to think of everything. Only a list helps so that the planned favorite food and drink is on board:

○ **Practical snacks for the journey** (apple slices, snack carrots, pretzel sticks ...)

○ **Drinking bottles for the journey**

○ **Breakfast** (bread & toppings / muesli & milk / oatmeal and fruit / juice etc.)

○ **Snacks for hikes** (hard-boiled eggs, cheese cubes, nuts, cherry tomatoes ...)

○ **Lunch, dinner** (ingredients / vegetable paste / herbs)

○ **Dessert** (yogurt / fruit / homemade ice cream)

○ **Coffee, tea, afternoon snack**

○ **Small sins** (chocolate ...)

○ **Wine, beer, spirits**

○ **Vinegar, olive oil** (only in winter, otherwise permanently on board)

○ **Perishable items from the refrigerator**

○ **Ripe fruit and vegetables from the (balcony) garden**

○ **Cookbook**

○ _____

Light Meals

<< 11 delicious recipes for summer days >>

Chili sin Carne

#FAST #VEGETARIAN #GLUTENFREE

1 cup **parboiled long grain rice** (7 oz.)
1 small **onion**
1 **clove of garlic**
1 **chili pepper** (alternatively chili powder)
2 tablespoons **olive oil**
1 can cooked **kidney beans** (15.5 oz.)
1 pack cooked **diced tomatoes** (14.5 oz.)
1 ½ cups **vegetable stock** (12 fl. oz.)
2 tablespoons **tomato paste**
2 teaspoons **sweet pepper powder**
1 teaspoon **cumin powder**
salt and **black pepper**
½ cup all natural **sour cream** (4 oz., alternatively natural yogurt)

➤ Bring rice with a little bit of salt to the boil with twice the amount of water. Then simmer the rice on low heat with the lid on, until all the water has been absorbed by the rice.

➤ Put on a disposable glove. Chop the onion, the clove of garlic and the chili pepper into small pieces. Wash the glove, take it off and hang it to dry. Heat olive oil in a large pot and cook the onions and the garlic in it using medium heat for 1 to 2 minutes. Drain the beans. Add tomatoes and kidney beans.

➤ Deglaze with the stock. Add tomato paste, pepper powder and cumin powder and simmer over low heat for 15 minutes with the lid on. Stir occasionally. Season to taste with salt and pepper. Serve the chili with the rice and a dollop of sour cream.

Shrimps with Zucchini and Parmesan

#ONEPOT #FISH #LOWCARB #GLUTENFREE

1 pack **shrimps** (9 oz., fresh or frozen and peeled)
2 **zucchini** (14 oz.)
1 small **onion**
1 **clove of garlic**
2 tablespoons **olive oil**
½ pot **whipped cream** (4 fl. oz., alternatively crème fraîche)
1 handful grated **Parmesan cheese** (2 oz.)
salt and **black pepper**

➤ If necessary, defrost the shrimps, put them in a sieve and wash off the protective glaze. Put on a disposable glove. Wash and clean the zucchini and cut it into bite-sized cubes. Peel and chop the onion and the garlic. Wash the glove, take it off and hang it to dry.

➤ Heat the olive oil in a pot and fry the shrimps, onions and garlic in it for about 1 minute over medium heat. Stir occasionally. Add zucchini and fry for another 2 minutes. Again stir occasionally.

➤ Deglaze everything with the cream, put on the lid and simmer for a few minutes. Season the meal with salt and pepper, serve in deep plates and add the Parmesan.

Shrimp Vegetables Avocado Pot

#ONEPOT #FISH #GLUTENFREE

1 pack **shrimps** (9 oz., fresh or frozen and peeled)
1 small **zucchini**
1 small **eggplant**
1 small **onion**
1 **clove of garlic**
1 pack cooked **diced tomatoes** (14.5 oz.)
a little bit of **water** (if necessary)
1 **avocado**
salt and **black pepper**
chili powder
1 handful grated **Parmesan** (2 oz.)

➤ Put the shrimps in the pot to defrost and steam them over low heat. Remove the shrimps and leave the water in the pot.

➤ Put on a disposable glove. Dice the zucchini, eggplant, onion and garlic and sauté in a pot. Wash the glove, take it off and hang it to dry. Deglaze with the tomatoes from the glass. Add a little water if necessary.

➤ Remove the peel and core from the avocado and cut into small pieces. At the end of the cooking time, add the avocado and shrimps. Wait until they warm up. Season with salt and a little pepper. Season to taste with chili. Scatter the Parmesan on top.

Stew with Chicken and Vegetables

#MEAT #GLUTENFREE

¾ cup **parboiled long grain rice** (4 oz.)
1 small **zucchini**
10 **cherry tomatoes**
1 **red sweet pointed pepper** (alternatively red bell pepper)
2 **cloves of garlic**
2 tablespoons **olive oil**
1 cup **tomato passata** (8 fl. oz.)
11 oz. **chopped chicken breast**
½ teaspoon **thyme**
½ teaspoon **oregano**
salt and **black pepper**

➤ Bring rice with a little bit of salt to the boil with twice the amount of water. Then simmer the rice on low heat with the lid on, until all the water has been absorbed by the rice.

➤ Put on a disposable glove. Wash the zucchini, cut into bite-sized pieces, and place in a cold pot. Wash cherry tomatoes and pepper, cut into bite-sized cubes, and add to the pot. Finely dice the garlic and add to the pot. Wash the glove, take it off and hang it to dry. Pour the olive oil over it and fry the vegetables for 2–3 minutes over medium heat.

➤ Deglaze the vegetables with the tomatoes. Put the chopped chicken in the pot and cook with them. Season with thyme, oregano and pepper. Simmer with the lid closed and low heat for about 20 minutes. Season with salt and serve with the rice.

Chicken Cauliflower Rice Pot

#ONEPOT #MEAT #LOWCARB #GLUTENFREE

2 **red sweet pointed peppers** (alternatively red bell peppers)
1 small **onion**
1 **clove of garlic**
11 oz. **chopped chicken** (alternatively chopped turkey)
2 tablespoons **olive oil**
1 pack (11 oz.) frozen **cauliflower rice** (alternatively fresh cauliflower)
1 handful of frozen **peas**
2 **eggs**
salt and **black pepper**
soy sauce

➤ Wash the peppers. Cut the onion, garlic and bell pepper into small pieces. Fry the chicken in the pot with the olive oil until it is through and lightly browned. Add the peppers, onions and garlic to the meat and fry for about 5 minutes over medium heat.

➤ If necessary, bring fresh cauliflower to rice grain size in the multi-chopper. Next, add the cauliflower rice and fry for about 3 minutes. Then add the peas.

➤ Whisk two eggs. Form a hole in the middle of the pot and pour the two whisked eggs into the hole. Let the eggs thicken and then stir everything together. Season the dish with salt, pepper and soy sauce.

Potato and Bell Pepper Stew with Cod

#ONEPOT #FISH #GLUTENFREE

1 small **onion**
1 **clove of garlic**
2 tablespoons **olive oil**
1 **yellow bell pepper**
1 pack of cooked **diced tomatoes** (14.5 oz.)
2 medium-sized **potatoes**
1 tablespoon **sweet pepper powder**
2 cups **vegetable stock** (17 fl. oz.)
salt and **black pepper**
fresh or frozen **cod** (11 oz.)

➤ If necessary, place the frozen fish fillet (in the foil) in warm water to thaw. Finely dice the onion and garlic and sauté both in a pot with the olive oil until translucent. Cut the bell pepper into small cubes and add to the pot. Add the diced tomatoes and fry everything for 5 minutes over medium heat.

➤ Peel the potatoes and cut them into bite-sized pieces. Add the potatoes, pepper powder, vegetable stock, salt and pepper. Simmer over low heat with the lid closed until the potatoes are cooked.

➤ Cut the cod into bite-sized pieces, add to the stew, and cook for another 10 minutes. At the end, season again with salt and serve hot.

Potato Goulash with Sauerkraut

#ONEPOT #VEGAN #GLUTENFREE

1 **onion**
2 tablespoons **olive oil**
1 **red pointed pepper** (alternatively red bell pepper)
floury **potatoes** (18 oz.)
2 tablespoons **tomato paste**
1 ⅔ cups **tomato passata** (14 fl. oz.)
⅔ cup **vegetable stock** (5 fl. oz.)
1 teaspoon **sweet pepper powder**
½ teaspoon **caraway seeds**
salt and **black pepper**
7 oz. **sauerkraut** (pasteurized)

➤ Finely dice the onion and sauté in olive oil until translucent. Cut the bell pepper into bite-sized pieces and sauté at low temperature. Wash and peel the potatoes and cut them into 1 cm cubes.

➤ Put the potato cubes and the tomato paste in the pot and let them roast briefly. Deglaze with the tomatoes and the stock. Add pepper powder, caraway seeds, salt and black pepper.

➤ Let the potato goulash simmer for about 40 minutes over a low heat, and stir now and then. When the potatoes are soft, add the sauerkraut, stir in and let it get hot. Season again with salt and black pepper.

ⓘ Cook this dish in double the amount. Then there will be no sauerkraut left, and the rest will taste heavenly the next day.

Salmon in Coconut Sauce with Broccoli

#FAST #FISH #LOWCARB #GLUTENFREE

3 fresh or frozen **salmon fillets** (11 oz.)
1 pack frozen **broccoli rice** (11 oz. alternatively fresh broccoli)
1 tablespoon **olive oil**
½ teaspoon **red curry paste**
1 small pack **coconut milk** (7.5 fl. oz.)
salt and **black pepper**
nutmeg

➤ If necessary, put the frozen fish fillet (in the foil) in warm water to thaw. If fresh broccoli is used, cut it to rice grain size with the multi-chopper.

➤ Steam the broccoli rice in a pot until it is thawed and cooked through. At the same time, pour a little bit of olive oil in a pan and briefly fry the salmon on all sides. Add the curry paste to the salmon and fry briefly. Then deglaze with <u>half </u>of the coconut milk and simmer on a low level. Season with salt.

➤ Meanwhile, add the other half of the coconut milk to the broccoli rice and season with salt, black pepper and nutmeg. Arrange the salmon with the sauce next to the broccoli rice on a plate.

Tomato Soup

1 **clove of garlic**
1 tablespoon **olive oil**
4 cup **tomato passata** (34 fl. oz.)
salt and **black pepper**
1 pinch **sugar**
⅔ cup **red wine** (4 fl. oz.)
1 tablespoon **white balsamic vinegar**
little bit **vegetable stock** or **water** if necessary
1 handful fresh **basil leaves**

➤ Finely dice the clove of garlic and fry briefly with olive oil in a pot. Before the garlic browns (and might get bitter), add the tomato passata and bring to the boil.

➤ Season to taste with salt, black pepper and sugar. Add red wine and vinegar, put on the lid and simmer for about 10 minutes. Season again to taste.

➤ If you want the soup to be thinner, you can add some vegetable stock or water. Roughly chop the basil. Put the soup in plates, sprinkle with basil and serve.

Zucchini with Tomatoes and Pine Nuts

#ONEPOT #VEGETARIAN #LOWCARB #GLUTENFREE

2 medium-sized **zucchini** (14 oz.)
2 **cloves of garlic**
2 tablespoons **pine nuts** (alternatively cedar nuts)
5 tablespoons **olive oil**
3 ⅓ **cups cherry tomatoes** (18 oz.)
1 tablespoon **tomato paste**
chili powder
salt and black **pepper**
1 handful fresh **basil leaves**
1 handful grated **Parmesan** (2 oz.)

➤ Put on a disposable glove. Cut the zucchinis into bite-sized pieces and place in a deep dish. Finely chop the garlic. Wash the glove, take it off and hang it to dry.

➤ In a large pot, briefly fry the garlic with the nuts in olive oil over medium heat. Add tomatoes and tomato paste. Let everything simmer for 2 minutes. Now add the zucchini and some chili, salt and pepper. Put the lid on and simmer for at least 10 minutes on a low heat. Stir occasionally. Chop the basil. Season again with the spices, distribute on deep plates and sprinkle the Parmesan and basil over the top.

ⓘ Also tastes good with pasta. In this case, only use about 250 g tomatoes. A dash of white wine in the sauce is also delicious.

Zucchini and Tomato Pot with Feta

#FAST #ONEPOT #VEGETARIAN #LOWCARB #GLUTENFREE

2 medium-sized **zucchini** (14 oz.)
2 tablespoons **olive oil**
3 **tomatoes** (14 oz.)
2 sprigs fresh **basil**
feta from sheep's milk (3,5 oz., already cut into pieces if available)
salt and **black pepper**

➤ Put on a disposable glove. Wash the zucchini and cut off the ends. Quarter lengthways, then cut into 3-5 mm thin slices and place in a cold pot. Wash the glove, take it off and hang it to dry. Pour the olive oil over the zucchini, stir and heat the pot. Fry the zucchini slices in it for about 5 minutes at medium heat, stirring occasionally.

➤ Wash the tomatoes, cut into large cubes, add and cook for 2 - 3 minutes.

➤ Pluck the basil leaves from the stems and add to the tomato and courgette vegetables, season with salt and black pepper. Dice the feta if necessary, add it and turn off the stove. The residual heat melts the feta and makes a creamy sauce.

Hearty Meals

<< 9 classic recipes for hungry cooks >>

Cabanossi Soup

#FAST #ONEPOT #MEAT #GLUTENFREE

1 pack **cabanossi** (8 oz., alternatively other sausages)
1 **clove of garlic**
1 **yellow bell pepper**
1 **red pointed pepper**
2 cups **vegetable stock** (17 fl. oz.)
1 small **onion**
1 small can **corn** (5 oz.)
1 small can cooked **kidney beans** (8 oz.)
1 pack cooked **diced tomatoes** (14.5 oz.)
½ cup all natural **sour cream** (4 oz., alternatively crème fraîche)
salt and **black pepper**
2 teaspoons **sweet pepper powder**

➤ Cut the sausages in thin slices. Finely dice the garlic. Wash the peppers and cut them into bite-sized pieces. Put the sausages, garlic, pepper and vegetable stock in a pot and bring to the boil.

➤ Peel the onion, dice it finely and put it in the pot. Drain the corn and kidney beans and add them to the pot as well. Add the chopped tomatoes. Cook the soup until the onions and peppers are soft.

➤ Finally, stir in the sour cream and season with black pepper, salt and pepper powder.

Barbecue Leftovers Pot

#FAST #ONEPOT #MEAT #GLUTENFREE

1 small **onion**
1 small **zucchini**
grilled meat or **grilled sausages**
2 tablespoons **tomato paste**
1 small can **corn** (5 oz.)
1 small can cooked **kidney beans** (8 oz.)
1 ⅓ cups **beef stock** (10 fl. oz.)
2 tablespoons **crème fraîche**
1 tablespoon **olive oil**
salt and **black pepper**

➤ Cut the onion into small cubes and fry them in a pot with olive oil. Put on a disposable glove. Cut the zucchini and the grilled meat into bite-sized pieces and place them in the pot.

➤ Wash the glove, take it off and hang it up to dry. Add the tomato paste, stir-fry briefly and deglaze with the stock.

➤ Drain the corn and beans, put them in the pot and bring to the boil. Stir in the crème fraîche and season with salt and black pepper.

Vegetables with Minced Meat

#ONEPOT #MEAT #LOWCARB #GLUTENFREE

1 **onion**
1 **red pointed pepper** (alternatively red bell pepper)
1 ⅓ cups **cherry tomatoes** (7 oz.)
2 tablespoons **olive oil**
minced beef (8 oz.)
salt and **pepper**
2 tablespoons **white balsamic vinegar**
grated **cheddar** (3,5 oz.)
fresh **parsley** (optional)

➤ Peel the onion and dice finely. Wash the pepper and cut it into 1 cm cubes. Wash and halve the tomatoes. Heat the olive oil in a pot and sauté the onion until translucent. Add minced beef and fry through.

➤ Add pepper and tomatoes, season everything with salt and black pepper, stir well and deglaze with vinegar. Put the lid on and simmer everything for about 8 minutes over medium heat. Stir occasionally.

➤ Sprinkle the cheddar over the food. Put the lid on for another 2 minutes until the cheese has melted. In the meantime, wash and chop the parsley. Divide the food on plates and sprinkle with the parsley.

Minced Meat Stew with Carrots

#ONEPOT #MEAT #LOWCARB #GLUTENFREE

1 medium-sized **onion**
1 **clove of garlic**
2 tablespoon **olive oil**
minced beef (8 oz., fresh or frozen)
3 medium-sized **carrots** (7 oz.)
5 teaspoons **tomato paste** (2,5 oz.)
1 ⅔ cups **beef stock** (14 fl. oz.)
1 **red pointed pepper**
1 handful **parsley** (optional)
salt and **black pepper**
2 tablespoons **crème fraîche** (optional)

➤ Peel the onion and garlic and dice them finely. Put the olive oil in a pot and fry the minced meat in it. Add onion and garlic. Wash the carrots, cut off the ends, quarter them, cut into thin slices and add to the minced meat. Fry everything for 5 minutes over medium heat, stirring occasionally.

➤ Add tomato paste and mix well. Then deglaze with the stock, bring to the boil and simmer covered for 20 minutes at low heat.

➤ Cut the peppers into small pieces and add them. Simmer the stew for another 10 minutes. Chop the parsley leaves and parsley stalks. Finally, season the stew with salt and black pepper. Arrange on deep plates and put parsley and a dollop of crème fraîche on each plate.

Minced Meat Pot with Vegetables and Mozzarella

#ONEPOT #MEAT #LOWCARB #GLUTENFREE

1 **onion**
2 **cloves of garlic**
olive oil
minced beef (8 oz.)
1 small **eggplant**
1 small **zucchini**
1 pack cooked **diced tomatoes** (14.5 oz.)
1 pack **mozzarella** (4,4 oz.)
all natural **cream cheese** (5 oz.)
salt and **black pepper**
1 handful fresh **basil leaves**

➤ Finely dice the onion and garlic. Heat olive oil in a pot and fry the onions and garlic briefly. Then add and fry the minced meat. Cut the eggplant into bite-sized cubes and add. Stir occasionally.

➤ Quarter the zucchini lengthways, cut them into bite-sized pieces and add them. Next, stir in the diced tomatoes and simmer briefly. Meanwhile, cut the mozzarella into small cubes.

➤ Stir in the cream cheese and season the food with salt and black pepper. Finally, place the mozzarella cubes on the vegetables and put a lid on the pot for about 5 minutes to melt the mozzarella. Arrange on plates and put basil on top.

Chicken in Sour Cream with Green Beans

#FAST #ONEPOT #MEAT #LOWCARB #GLUTENFREE

olive oil
chopped chicken (14 oz.)
1 jar **green beans** (6.5 oz. drained weight)
salt and **black pepper**
1 teaspoon **sweet pepper powder**
1 pot all natural **sour cream** (8 oz., alternatively crème fraîche)

➤ Let olive oil get hot in a pot and fry the chopped chicken in it until it browns. Meanwhile, put the lid on and allow the beans to drain. Season the meat with black pepper, salt and pepper powder.

➤ Reduce the heat, add the drained beans to the meat and let them warm up. Stir gently so that the beans don't break.

➤ After 1–2 minutes, add the sour cream and bring to the boil briefly. Season again with the spices and serve.

Cheese Fondue from the Pan

#FAST #ONEPOT #VEGETARIAN

1 large or 2 small **Camembert** (mild)
1 **baguette**
1 **red pointed pepper** (alternatively red bell pepper)
2 **carrots**
½ **cucumber**
1 handful **of grapes** (optional)

➤ Take the Camembert cheese out of the packaging and place it in the pan. Put the lid on the pan and heat the cheese on the lowest heat for 20 to 25 minutes. In the meantime, cut the baguette into slices and the vegetables into sticks. The cheese is ready when its top and side walls begin to bulge and give way slightly when pressed with a finger.

➤ Serve the Camembert in the pan or lift it out of the pan and place it on a plate. Cut the lid of the Camemberts crosswise with a sharp knife and fold the 4 corners outwards. Dip the baguette and vegetable sticks into the liquid cheese. Snack on the grapes.

ⓘ Grill cheese from the cooling shelf can also be wonderfully melted in a coated pan and is a delicious accompaniment to salads or snacks.

Mexican Bowl

#ONEPOT #MEAT #GLUTENFREE

1 **onion**
2 tablespoons **olive oil**
chopped **chicken** (11 oz.)
1 ⅓ cups **poultry** stock (10 fl. oz.)
1 pack cooked **diced tomatoes** (14.5 oz.)
1 small can **corn** (approx. 150 g)
1 small can cooked **kidney beans** (8 oz.)
1 teaspoon **sweet pepper powder**
½ teaspoon **cumin powder**
½ teaspoon **chili powder**
½ cup **parboiled long grain rice** (3.5 oz.)
grated **Gouda** (2.6 oz., medium-old)
salt and **black pepper**
½ cup all natural **sour cream** (4 oz., alternatively crème fraîche)

➤ Finely dice the onion and fry it in a little olive oil until translucent. Put the chicken strips in the pot. Add the chicken stock, diced tomatoes, corn and kidney beans. Season with paprika powder, cumin and chili. Then bring to the boil. Add the rice, making sure that it is completely covered with the stock. Put the lid on and stir occasionally.

➤ Grate the Gouda. Let the rice simmer until it has absorbed the liquid. Season to taste with salt and pepper.

➤ Switch off the stove and sprinkle the contents of the pot with the Gouda. Put the lid on and wait for the Gouda to melt. Stir the sour cream in the cup and pour it on the cheese in blobs. Serve in deep plates.

Oriental Minced Meat Pot

#ONEPOT #MEAT #GLUTENFREE

2 tablespoons **pine nuts** (alternatively cedar nuts)
1 **clove of garlic**
2 tablespoon **olive oil**
minced meat (9 oz. lamb or beef)
1 teaspoon **"Ras el Hanout" spice mixture**
½ **leek**
2 **red pointed peppers**
1 tablespoon **raisins**
⅓ cup **water** (2.5 fl. oz.)
salt and **black pepper**
a little **coriander green** or flat leaf **parsley**
2 medium-sized **tomatoes**
¼ **cucumber**
Greek yogurt (5 oz., cream yogurt)

➤ Roast the nuts in a pot without oil. Take out the nuts and set aside. Meanwhile, dice the garlic, then clean the leek. Halve the white or light green part of the leek and cut into thin slices.

➤ Heat olive oil in a pot and fry the minced meat in it. Add the diced garlic and ras el hanout and fry briefly. Clean the pepper and cut it into 5 mm thick, bite-sized strips. Add the leek, pepper and raisins to the pot and fry for 5 minutes. Add the water, bring everything to the boil, season with salt and black pepper and simmer over medium heat for about 10 minutes.

➤ Pluck the coriander or parsley leaves, roughly chop them and set it aside. Dice the tomato and add to the pot. Peel the cucumber and also dice it. Mix the cucumber cubes with the yogurt and season with salt and black pepper. Put the food in plates, sprinkle with coriander leaves and the roasted pine nuts and serve with the cucumber yogurt.

Pasta Dishes

<< 8 good mood recipes for every day >>

Pasta alla Putanesca

#ONEPOT #FISH

1 **onion**
1 **clove of garlic**
anchovies (1 oz., canned, in olive oil)
2 tablespoons **olive oil**
2 cups **vegetable stock** (17 fl. oz.)
2 tablespoons **tomato paste**
½ teaspoon **chili powder**
2 cups **fusilli** (7 oz., pasta of durum wheat semolina)
1 cup **cherry tomatoes** (5 oz.)
5 **black olives** (seedless, e.g. Kalamon or Kalamata)
salt and **black pepper**
½ teaspoon **oregano**
½ teaspoon **thyme**
1 handful fresh **basil leaves**

➤ Cut onion, garlic and anchovies into small pieces. In a pot, sauté the onion with olive oil until translucent. Pour the vegetable stock on top. Add garlic, anchovies, tomato paste and chili powder and bring to the boil. Add the pasta, put the lid on, simmer over low heat and stir occasionally. If the sauce is too thin, let it cook without the lid.

➤ Halve the cherry tomatoes and finely chop the olives. Stir in tomatoes and olives as soon as the pasta is al dente. Season to taste with salt, black pepper, oregano and thyme. Chop the basil and sprinkle the served food with it.

Pasta in Bolognese Sauce

#ONEPOT #MEAT

2 tablespoons **olive oil**
1 **clove of garlic**
1 small **onion**
minced meat (9 oz. fresh or frozen)
1 ½ cup **tomato passata** (12 fl. oz.)
1 ⅓ cups **beef stock** (10 fl. oz.)
½ teaspoon **oregano**
½ teaspoon **rosemary**
2 teaspoons **tomato paste**
salt and **black pepper**
1 ½ cups **fusilli** (5.6 oz., pasta of durum wheat semolina)
1 handful grated **Parmesan** (2 oz.)

➤ If frozen, place the minced meat in the plastic foil in warm water and defrost it. Finely dice the garlic and onion and sauté in a pot with olive oil until translucent.

➤ Add the minced meat and stir-fry occasionally. Add the tomato passata and the stock. Add the oregano, rosemary and tomato paste. Season to taste with salt and black pepper. Let everything boil.

➤ Add the pasta. Stir frequently and simmer over low heat to prevent the pasta from sticking to the bottom. As soon as the pasta is done, turn off the stove. Divide the food on deep plates and sprinkle with Parmesan.

Pasta with Avocado and Cream Cheese

#SCHNELL #VEGETARIAN

3 cups **fusilli** (10.5 oz., pasta of durum wheat semolina)
salt
2 tablespoons **pine nuts** (alternatively cedar nuts)
½ **lemon**
1 ripe **avocado**
½ pack all natural **cream cheese** (2.6 oz.)

➤ Cook the pasta in salted water. Roast the nuts in a pan without oil. Squeeze the lemon. Halve the avocado, remove the stone and remove it from the skin with a tablespoon.

➤ Mix the avocado with the cream cheese, a little salt and lemon juice in a bowl with a fork and season to taste.

➤ Drain the pasta. Add the pasta and the avocado cream cheese sauce to the pot and mix. Put the pasta in plates and sprinkle with the nuts.

Pasta with Mushrooms and Kohlrabi

#ONEPOT #VEGETARIAN

1 **kohlrabi** (7 oz.)
½ **leek**
1 ½ cups **fusilli** (5.6 oz., pasta of durum wheat semolina)
1 ⅓ cups **water** (9 fl. oz.)
1 cup **milk** (7 fl. oz.)
10 **mushrooms** (5.6 oz., fresh or frozen)
2 tablespoons all natural **cream cheese**
salt and **black pepper**
nutmeg

➤ Peel the kohlrabi and cut it into small cubes. Wash and quarter the leek and cut it into fine strips.

➤ Put the kohlrabi, leek and fusilli in a pot with water and milk. Bring to the boil and stir well. Continue simmering over medium heat.

➤ Clean the mushrooms if necessary, cut into slices and add. Simmer for 10 to 15 minutes until the desired consistency. Stir occasionally. When the pasta is al dente, season with cream cheese, salt, black pepper and nutmeg.

Pasta with Salmon and Kohlrabi

#ONEPOT #FISH

2 **kohlrabies** (14 oz.)
1 **onion**
2 **salmon fillets** (9 oz.)
olive oil
1 pot **whipped cream** (8 fl. oz., alternatively crème fraîche)
2 cups **vegetable stock** (17 fl. oz.)
2 ½ cups **fusilli** (9 oz., pasta of durum wheat semolina)
salt and **black pepper**

➤ Peel the kohlrabi and cut into small cubes. Peel the onion and chop finely. Cut the salmon into bite-sized cubes. If present, remove the skin from the salmon.

➤ Sauté the onion in olive oil in a pot. As soon as the onion is translucent, add the kohlrabi and cook for about 3 minutes. Add the cream and stock and bring to the boil. Add the fusilli and simmer over low heat for about 15 minutes until the pasta is cooked through. Stir occasionally so that nothing burns to the bottom.

➤ As soon as the pasta is al dente, add the salmon to the pot and let it simmer. Season to taste with salt and black pepper.

Pasta with Parmesan and Spinach

#ONEPOT #VEGETARIAN

1 small **onion**
1 **clove of garlic**
2 tablespoons **pine nuts** (alternatively cedar nuts)
2 cups **fusilli** (7 oz., pasta of durum wheat semolina)
frozen **spinach leaves** (9 oz.)
salt and **black pepper**
2 cups **vegetable stock** (17 fl. oz.)
½ pot **whipped cream** (4 fl. oz., alternatively crème fraîche)
1 handful fresh **basil leaves**
1 handful grated **Parmesan** (2 oz.)

➤ Peel and finely dice the onion and clove of garlic. Roast the nuts in a pan without oil.

➤ Put the pasta in a pot with the frozen spinach, onion, garlic, salt, black pepper, stock and whipped cream. Put the lid on, simmer over low heat and stir now and then. Chop the basil leaves into small pieces.

➤ If necessary, add water to the pot and simmer the food until the pasta is cooked through. Stir in the basil and nuts. Season the meal with salt, place in deep plates, sprinkle with Parmesan and serve.

Pasta with Smoked Salmon and Asparagus

#ONEPOT #FISH

green asparagus (18 oz.)
½ **leek** (2 oz.)
2 cups **fusilli** (7 oz., pasta of durum wheat semolina)
2 cups **vegetable stock** (14 fl. oz.)
1 cup **cherry tomatoes** (5 oz.)
1 pack **smoked salmon** (7 oz.)
salt and **black pepper**

➤ Cut off the woody part of the asparagus at the bottom. Cut the asparagus stalks into pieces of approx. 3 cm length. Cut the leek into thin strips.

➤ Put the asparagus, pasta, leek and stock in a pot. Simmer with the lid closed for about 10 minutes, stirring regularly in between. Wash and halve the tomatoes. Cut the salmon into small pieces.

➤ When the pasta is done and most of the liquid has absorbed, add the tomatoes and salmon and let them warm up. Season to taste with salt and pepper.

Pasta with Tuna

#FAST #ONEPOT #FISH

1 can **tuna** in its own juice
1 ⅓ cups **vegetable stock** (10 fl. oz.)
2 tablespoons **crème fraîche**
2 ½ cups **fusilli** (9 oz., pasta of durum wheat semolina)
1 pack cooked **diced tomatoes** (14.5 oz.)
1 tablespoon **white balsamic vinegar**
salt and **black pepper**
chili powder
2 tablespoons **tomato paste**
1 handful fresh **basil leaves**

➤ Drain the tuna juice. Put the tuna in a pot and roughly mash it. Put all ingredients, except the basil, in a pot and bring to the boil with the lid closed. Then simmer over low heat until the pasta is cooked through.

➤ Stir regularly so that the pasta does not burn on the base. Add liquid if necessary.

➤ As soon as the pasta is cooked, season again with salt and pepper. Stir in half of the basil leaves and use the rest to garnish.

Kid-friendly Meal Ideas

<< 10 popular recipes for the young ones on board >>

Chopped Turkey in Pineapple Sauce with Rice

#FAST #MEAT #GLUTENFREE

1 cup **parboiled long grain rice** (7 oz.)
2 tablespoons **almond flakes**
1 tablespoon **olive oil**
1 tablespoon **water**
chopped turkey (9 oz.)
½ pot **whipped cream** (4 fl. oz., alternatively crème fraîche)
½ cup **pineapple chunks** (3.5 oz. drained weight)
⅔ cup **chicken stock** (4 fl. oz.)
1 teaspoon **curry powder**
salt and **black pepper**

➤ Bring rice with a little bit of salt to the boil with twice the amount of water. Then simmer the rice on low heat with the lid on, until all the water has been absorbed by the rice.

➤ Briefly roast the almond flakes in a pot without oil and place in a small bowl. Then add olive oil and water to the pot and fry the meat in it.

➤ As soon as the meat is cooked through, add the cream and stock. Season with curry. Add the pineapple pieces and briefly bring the curry to the boil. Season to taste with salt and black pepper. Serve with the rice on deep plates. Top with the roasted almond flakes.

ⓘ If part of the oil is replaced by water (still or carbonated), there will be less irritating fat vapor and the meat will be more tender.

Stew with Vienna Sausages and Vegetables

#ONEPOT #MEAT #GLUTENFREE

1 **onion**
3 medium-sized **potatoes** (11 oz.)
3 medium-sized **carrots** (9 oz.)
1 **kohlrabi**
1 tablespoon **butter**
4 cups **poultry stock** (34 fl. oz.)
salt and **black pepper**
4 **Vienna sausages** (7 oz.)

➤ Peel and finely dice the onion. Wash the potatoes if necessary, then peel and cut into 1 cm cubes. Wash the carrots if necessary and cut into thin quarters. Peel the kohlrabi and cut into 1 cm cubes.

➤ Melt the butter in a pot and sauté the onion until translucent. Add the remaining vegetables and sauté briefly. Then pour in the stock. Season the stew with salt and black pepper and simmer until the vegetables are soft. Meanwhile, halve the Vienna sausages and cut them into small pieces.

➤ Then switch off the stove. Put the Vienna sausages in the stew and heat them up. Season the stew again with salt and pepper. Spread the stew on deep plates.

ⓘ For our son, we cut the Vienna sausages halfways and into very small pieces. So he cannot choke on it and eats the sausage pieces together with the remaining ingredients instead of picking them out individually.

Chickpea Stew with Chicken

#ONEPOT #MEAT #GLUTENFREE

1 small **onion**
1 **clove of garlic**
1 medium-sized **zucchini**
1 tablespoon **olive oil**
chopped chicken (6 oz.)
1 ⅓ cups **poultry stock** (10 fl. oz.)
⅔ cup **tomato passata** (5 fl. oz.)
4 tablespoons **red lentils**
2 tablespoons **raisins**
1 teaspoon **honey**
1 tablespoon **tomato paste**
salt and **black pepper**
1 glass **chickpeas** (8 oz. drained weight)

➤ Peel the onion and garlic and cut into small cubes. Wash the zucchini, remove the ends and cut into 0.5-1 cm small cubes. Heat the olive oil in the pot and fry the chopped chicken with the lid on. Stir occasionally.

➤ Next add onion and garlic and sauté briefly. Deglaze with the stock and add the tomatoes. Then add the lentils, zucchini, raisins, honey and tomato paste. Season to taste with salt and black pepper.

➤ Simmer for 10 minutes, stirring occasionally. Drain the chickpeas, add them and let them warm up. Finally, season again to taste.

Chicken Stock with Alphabet Noodles

#ONEPOT #FAST

4 cups **chicken stock / poultry stock** (34 fl. oz.)
1 **carrot**
At choice **alphabet noodles / soup noodles**
1 **egg**
salt

➤ Heat stock in a pot. Meanwhile, cut the carrot lengthways into 4 strips and then into approx. 2 mm thin slices. As soon as the stock simmers, add the carrot pieces and the desired amount of pasta.

➤ Simmer at a low temperature until the pasta and carrots are soft. Whisk an egg and add to the stock while stirring. Season to taste with a little salt.

Kohlrabi & Pea Stew with Vienna Sausages

#ONEPOT #FAST #GLUTENFREE

2 **kohlrabi**
2 **medium-sized potatoes**
1 cups **vegetable stock** (8 fl. oz.)
4 **Vienna sausages** (7 oz.)
13 tablespoons frozen **peas** (5 oz., alternatively ½ glas)
½ pot **whipped cream** (4 fl. oz., alternatively crème fraîche)
salt and **black pepper**

➤ Peel the kohlrabi and the potatoes and cut it into small pieces of about 1 cm length. Simmer the vegetable stock, the cubed kohlrabi and potatoes in a pot with a lit for 10 minutes. Meanwhile, halve the Vienna sausages and cut them into thin slices.

➤ Put the Vienna sausages and peas in the pot and simmer for another 10 minutes. Add the cream, bring to the boil briefly, then switch off. Season everything with a little salt and black pepper.

ⓘ For our son, we cut the Vienna sausages halfways and into very small pieces. So he cannot choke on it and eats the sausage pieces together with the remaining ingredients instead of picking them out individually.

Noodle Pot with Vienna Sausages

#FAST #ONEPOT #MEAT

2 tablespoons **butter**
2 tablespoons **flour**
2 tablespoon **tomato paste**
2 cups **vegetable stock** (17 fl. oz.)
1 ⅔ cup **tomato passata** (14 fl. oz.)
salt
⅔ cup **alphabet noodles** (7 oz.)
4 **Vienna sausages** (7 oz.)

➤ Melt the butter in a pot. Stir in flour, stir in tomato paste and sauté briefly. Deglaze with vegetable stock and tomato passata. Add ½ teaspoon salt. Add the alphabet noodles and simmer over low heat, stirring occasionally.

➤ Add a little more vegetable stock if necessary. When the pasta is done, turn off the stove. Halve the Vienna sausages and cut into slices, add to the stew and let it warm up. Season with salt again before serving.

ⓘ For our son, we cut the Vienna sausages halfways and into very small pieces. So he cannot choke on it and eats the sausage pieces together with the remaining ingredients instead of picking them out individually.

Pasta with Mushroom Sauce

#ONEPOT #VEGETARIAN

3 cups **mushrooms** (9 oz., fresh or frozen)
2 tablespoons **olive oil**
1 **onion**
1 **clove of garlic**
salt and **black pepper**
½ teaspoon **sweet pepper powder**
1 tablespoon **tomato paste**
2 cups **vegetable stock** (17 fl. oz.)
1 pot **whipped cream** (8 fl. oz., alternatively crème fraîche)
2 cups **fusilli** (7 oz., pasta of durum wheat semolina)
1 teaspoon **rosemary**
½ teaspoon **thyme**
1 handful grated **Parmesan** (2 oz.)

➤ Clean the mushrooms, cut them in half and then into 5 mm thin slices. Fry the mushrooms in a pot with a little olive oil. Cut the onion and garlic into small cubes and add to the pot. Season with salt, black pepper and sweet pepper powder.

➤ Sauté the tomato paste and then deglaze with the stock and cream. Add the fusilli, rosemary and thyme. Put the lid on and let everything simmer over low heat until the noodles are cooked through. Stir again and again in between so that the noodles do not stick to each other or to the bottom. Add water if necessary.

➤ Reduce the heat more and more, the softer the pasta is cooked and the less liquid there is. When the pasta is al dente, the sauce should be nice and creamy. Season again if necessary. Pour into deep plates and sprinkle with Parmesan cheese.

Pasta with Shrimps and Tomatoes

#ONEPOT #FISH

1 small **onion**
1 ⅔ cups **cherry tomatoes** (9 oz.)
1 **clove of garlic**
2 ½ cups **fusilli** (9 oz., durum wheat semolina)
1 pack **shrimps** (9 oz., fresh or frozen and peeled)
3 tablespoons **olive oil**
2 cups **vegetable stock** (17 fl. oz.)
salt
2 stalks fresh **basil**
Some coarsely grated **cheese** (e.g. Gouda)

➤ Thaw the shrimps, if necessary, put them in a colander and wash off the protective glaze. Peel the onion and chop finely. Wash and halve the tomatoes. Peel the garlic and cut into thin cubes.

➤ Put the pasta with tomatoes, garlic, onions, shrimps and the olive oil in a pot. Add vegetable stock. Bring everything to the boil, then reduce the heat and simmer gently for about 15 minutes with the lid on.

➤ Stir occasionally and cook until the pasta is al dente and most of the liquid has gone. Season to taste with salt. Cut the basil leaves into strips. Arrange the pasta on plates and top with the basil and grated cheese.

Pasta Napoli

#FAST #ONEPOT #VEGAN

1 small **onion**
1 tablespoon **olive oil**
3 tablespoon **tomato paste**
1 pack cooked **diced tomatoes** (14.5 oz.)
2 ⅓ cups **vegetable stock** (20 fl. oz.)
1 tablespoon **white balsamic vinegar**
salt and **black pepper**
½ teaspoon **oregano**
1 pinch **thyme**
2 ½ cups **fusilli** (9 oz., pasta of durum wheat semolina)
1 handful fresh **basil leaves**

➤ Peel the onion, dice it finely and sauté briefly in a pot with olive oil until translucent. Add the tomato paste and roast briefly. Deglaze with the diced tomatoes, stock and vinegar. Season with salt, black pepper, oregano and thyme.

➤ Put the pasta in the pot, stir regularly and simmer over a low heat until cooked. Add salt if necessary. Divide the pasta on deep plates and garnish with basil leaves.

Pan Pizza

12 **cherry tomatoes**
3 cups **Gouda** (9 oz., grated or straight)
4 big-sized **tortillas**
12 tablespoons **tomato passata**
salt and **black pepper**
oregano
1 handful fresh **basil leaves**

➤ Cut the cherry tomatoes in small slices. Grate Gouda if necessary. Place 1 tortilla in a pan and heat over low heat. In the meantime, spread 2–3 tablespoons of tomato passata on the tortilla, leaving 1 cm free at the edges.

➤ Season with salt, black pepper and oregano. Put on the tomato slices and sprinkle with Gouda cheese. Make sure that no topping runs under the tortilla and burns.

➤ Now heat the pan pizza for a few minutes over low heat until the cheese melts. Finally, sprinkle with basil leaves. Serve the pan pizza on a flat plate, cut into eighths, and prepare the next pizza.

Asian Dishes

<< 14 exotic recipes for aromatic treats >>

Asian Curry with Chicken

#ONEPOT #MEAT #GLUTENFREE

1 small **onion**
1 **clove of garlic**
½ stick **leek**
1 medium-sized **carrot** (alternatively bell pepper or spinach)
chopped chicken (11 oz., alternatively minced chicken)
2 tablespoons light **sesame oil** (alternatively peanut oil)
1 ⅔ cups **vegetable stock** (14 fl. oz.)
1 small pack **coconut milk** (7.5 fl. oz.)
6 tablespoons **parboiled long grain rice** (1.8 oz.)
salt and **black pepper**
½ teaspoon **red curry paste**
1 tablespoon fresh **ginger**
1 pinch **turmeric**
1 tablespoon **lime juice** (alternatively lime juice)

➤ Peel and finely dice onion, garlic and ginger. Cut the leek into small pieces and the carrot into fine strips 2-3 cm long.

➤ Heat the oil in a large pot and fry the meat in it. Add the vegetables and sauté briefly. Pour salt, black pepper, curry paste, ginger and turmeric over it. Fry everything briefly and then deglaze with the stock and coconut milk.

➤ Add the rice, put the lid on the pot, stir occasionally and simmer everything over a low heat until the rice is cooked through. Season to taste with lemon juice and add salt if necessary. Serve hot.

Ayurvedic Curry with Sweet Potatoes

#ONEPOT #VEGETARIAN #GLUTENFREE

1 small **onion**
1 **clove of garlic**
1 tablespoon fresh **ginger**
1 tablespoon **ghee** (alternatively 2 tablespoons olive oil)
1 small **sweet potato** (7 oz.)
½ teaspoon **chili powder**
½ teaspoon **garam masala spice mix** (optional)
⅔ cup **vegetable stock** (4 fl. oz.)
1 small pack **coconut milk** (7.5 fl. oz.)
1 glass of **chickpeas** (8 oz. drained weight)
50 g fresh or frozen **spinach**
½ **lemon**
salt and **black pepper**
2 tablespoons **cashew nuts**

➤ Cut the onion, garlic and ginger into small cubes and sauté in a pot with ghee for 2 minutes over medium heat. Peel the sweet potato and cut into small cubes. Put the sweet potato in the pot. Add chili powder and garam masala, stir continuously and fry for 1–2 minutes.

➤ Add the vegetable stock and coconut milk and bring to the boil. Reduce the heat and put the lid on. Wash the spinach and chickpeas. When the sweet potato is done, add the chickpeas and spinach, stir in and let warm. Turn off the stove. Season to taste with 2 tablespoons of lemon juice, salt and pepper. Place in two deep plates, sprinkle with cashew nuts and serve.

Chicken Korma with Cauliflower Rice

#LOWCARB #MEAT #GLUTENFREE

1 pack frozen **cauliflower rice** (10.5 oz., alternatively fresh cauliflower)

1 small **onion**

1 **clove of garlic**

1 teaspoon **tomato paste**

1 tablespoon **ghee** (alternatively olive oil)

1 teaspoon **garam masala spice mix**

1 teaspoon **cumin powder**

1 teaspoon **coriander powder**

1 teaspoon **sweet pepper powder**

½ teaspoon **turmeric powder**

1 teaspoon fresh **ginger**

chopped chicken (11 oz.)

1 small pack **coconut milk** (7.5 fl. oz.)

Salt and **black pepper**

► Take the cauliflower rice out of the freezer and start to thaw it. If necessary, bring fresh cauliflower to rice grain size in the multi-chopper. Peel onion and garlic and chop finely. Melt the ghee in a pot. Add onions, garlic, ginger and all the spices and sauté for 2 minutes while stirring over medium heat. Now add the meat and coconut milk and let everything simmer for 20 minutes. Season to taste with salt and pepper.

► About 10 minutes before serving, place the cauliflower rice in a pan. Roast in the pan without adding fat or water (with 2 tablespoons of water for fresh cauliflower), season with salt and pepper and serve with the curry.

Peanut Curry with Chicken

#ONEPOT #MEAT #GLUTENFREE

chopped chicken (7 oz.)
4 tablespoons **peanut oil**
1 **onion**
1 ½ cups **potatoes** (7.5 oz., semi-waxy)
1 pack **coconut milk** (14 fl. oz.)
2 tablespoons **red curry paste**
2 tablespoons **peanut butter** with peanut pieces (sugar-free)
1 teaspoon **sugar**
2 tablespoons **soy sauce**
1 teaspoon **lime**
1 **sweet pointed pepper** (alternatively red bell pepper)
½ **lime**
½ cup **peanuts** (2 oz.)
fresh **coriander**

➤ Heat a little peanut oil in a pot. Add the chopped chicken, lightly salt and fry with the lid closed. Meanwhile, finely dice the onion and cut the potatoes into bite-sized pieces. Take the meat out of the pot.

➤ Put more peanut oil in the pot and heat it up. Fry the onion in it until translucent. Add coconut milk, stir in curry paste, peanut butter, sugar and soy sauce. Rub the lime zest and add. Add the potatoes and simmer over low heat until cooked, meaning they can be easily divided with a spoon or knife. Stir occasionally.

➤ Cut the pointed peppers into cubes, add as soon as the potatoes are cooked and cook for another 3 minutes. Finally, put the meat back in the pot and briefly bring to the boil again. Season to taste with lime juice. Chop the peanuts and coriander to garnish the dish.

Fish Coconut Curry

2 **fish fillets** (9 oz., fresh or frozen, e.g. cod, saithe, halibut)
1 tablespoon fresh **ginger**
1 small **onion**
2 **cloves of garlic**
1 red **chili**
3 stalks **coriander greens**
1 large **tomato**
2 tablespoon light **sesame oil**
1 tablespoon **cumin powder**
1 tablespoon **coriander powder**
1 tablespoon **turmeric powder**
1 pack **coconut milk** (14 fl. oz.)
salt

➤ If necessary, put the frozen fish fillet (in the foil) in warm water to thaw. Cut the ginger, onion, garlic and chili pepper into small cubes. Roughly chop the coriander leaves, cut the tomato into cubes and set aside.

➤ Let the sesame oil get hot in a pot and briefly fry the ginger, onion, garlic and chili in it. Add cumin powder, coriander powder and turmeric powder and lightly roast for a few seconds, stirring constantly over medium heat. Pour the coconut milk on top and let the sauce boil down for approx. 5 minutes over a low heat.

➤ In the meantime, cut the fish into bite-sized pieces. Season the sauce in the pot well with salt and add the fish. The fish is done in 3 minutes. Now add the tomato, it should only get hot. Season with salt again, place on a plate and garnish with fresh coriander leaves.

Fish with Vegetables in Coconut Milk

#ONEPOT #FISH #LOWCARB #GLUTENFREE

2 **fish fillets** (9 oz., fresh or frozen, e.g. cod, saithe, halibut)
2 tablespoon light **sesame oil**
1 medium-sized **onion**
1 **clove of garlic**
1 tablespoon fresh **ginger**
2 **bell peppers** (red and orange/yellow)
1 **broccoli** (fresh or frozen, edible portion approx. 350 g)
1 pack **coconut milk** (14 fl. oz.)
salt and **black pepper**

➤ If necessary, put the frozen fish fillet (in the foil) in warm water to thaw. Put the sesame oil in the pot. Wash the vegetables. Finely dice the onion, garlic and ginger, coarsely dice the bell peppers, divide fresh broccoli into florets.

➤ Fry the vegetables, except for the broccoli, in the sesame oil over a medium heat. Put the lid on and stir occasionally. After 5 minutes, pour in the coconut milk and simmer for about 5 minutes on a low flame.

➤ Season to taste with salt and pepper. Then add the broccoli. Simmer for about 5 minutes, then cut the fish into small pieces, add and simmer again for about 5 minutes until the fish is cooked through. Serve the food in deep plates.

ⓘ If you want, you can cook a cup of rice or add glass noodles to the curry. Then it is no longer low carb, but also very tasty.

Shrimps and Coconut Soup

#ONEPOT #FISH #GLUTENFREE

1 small pack of **shrimps** (4.5 oz., fresh or frozen and peeled)
1 **clove of garlic**
1 teaspoon fresh **ginger**
½ stick **leek**
2 medium-sized **carrots** (approx. 150 g)
2 tablespoons light **sesame oil**
1 teaspoon **red curry paste**
1 ⅓ cups **vegetable stock** (10 fl. oz.)
1 small pack **coconut milk** (7.5 fl. oz.)
1 **lemon juice**
salt and **black pepper**

➤ If necessary, defrost the shrimps, put them in a sieve and wash off the protective glaze. Peel and finely chop the garlic and ginger. Clean and wash the leek and cut into rings. Clean, wash and peel the carrots, cut lengthways into strips, then dice finely.

➤ Put the sesame oil in a pot. Add the ginger and garlic and fry for 1 - 2 minutes over a medium heat. Add the curry paste, carrots and leek and sauté for 2 - 5 minutes while stirring. Pour in the stock and coconut milk. Bring to the boil and simmer until the vegetables are cooked through.

➤ Squeeze out the lemon juice. Season the soup with lemon juice, salt and pepper. Add the shrimps to the soup and let them cook until done. Serve in deep plates.

Chickpeas Tikka Masala

#ONEPOT #VEGETARIAN #GLUTENFREE

1 **onion**
1 **clove of garlic**
1 tablespoon fresh **ginger**
1 medium-sized **potato** (5 oz., semi-waxy)
1 tablespoon **ghee** (alternatively 2 tablespoons olive oil)
1 teaspoon **curry powder**
½ teaspoon **garam masala spice mix**
½ teaspoon **cumin powder**
1 pack of cooked **diced tomatoes** (14.5 oz.)
1 glass of **chickpeas** (8 oz. drained weight)
1 pack **spinach** (7 oz., frozen)
1 small pack **coconut milk** (7.5 fl. oz.)
½ **lemon**
salt and **black pepper**

➤ Peel the onion, garlic, ginger and potatoes and dice them. Melt ghee in a pot and sauté the onion in it. As soon as the onion is translucent, add the garlic, ginger, curry powder, garam masala and cumin and roast for about 30 seconds. Stir constantly. Deglaze with the diced tomatoes. Add potatoes. Let the curry simmer for about 10 minutes with the lid closed and low heat. Stir occasionally.

➤ Drain the chickpeas. Add the chickpeas and spinach to the pot and simmer over a low heat for another 20 minutes. Stir occasionally.

➤ When the potatoes are done, add the coconut milk, bring to the boil and then switch off the stove. Squeeze the lemon. Season the curry with salt, pepper and lemon juice.

Chickpea Curry

#FAST #ONEPOT #VEGAN #GLUTENFREE

1 large **potato** (9 oz., semi-waxy)
2 medium-sized **carrots** (7 oz.)
salt
1 **clove of garlic**
1 glass **chickpeas** (8 oz. drained weight)
1 small can of **corn** (5 oz.)
1 tablespoon **tomato paste**
1 tablespoon **curry powder**
1 teaspoon **chili powder**
½ teaspoon **coriander powder**
½ teaspoon **cumin powder**
1 cup **tomato passata** (8 fl. oz.)
1 small pack **coconut milk** (7.5 fl. oz.)

➤ Peel the potatoes and carrots and cut into cubes 1-2 cm in size. Pour into a pot and fill in some water so that the potatoes and carrots are not completely covered. Lightly salt the water. Put the lid on and simmer the vegetables in the salted water until they are cooked, and the water has reduced significantly.

➤ Finely dice the garlic and place in the pot. Drain the chickpeas and corn and add. Add the tomato paste, curry powder, chili powder, coriander and cumin and stir well.

➤ Add the tomatoes and coconut milk. Simmer on low heat for 10 minutes. Season again with chili and salt.

Mango Curry with Chicken

#ONEPOT #MEAT #GLUTENFREE

minced chicken (9 oz., alternatively chopped poultry)
1 small **onion**
2 **bell peppers** (red and yellow)
1 medium-sized **zucchini**
1 tablespoon **ghee** (alternatively 2 tablespoons olive oil)
2 teaspoons **red curry paste**
2 teaspoons **tomato paste**
1 small pack **coconut milk** (7.5 fl. oz.)
⅔ cup **vegetable stock** (5 fl. oz.)
salt and **black pepper**
1 ripe **mango**

➤ Defrost the minced poultry if necessary. Cut the onion into small cubes and place in the cold pot. Cut the bell peppers into small pieces and set aside. Put on a disposable glove. Wash the zucchini, cut into bite-sized pieces, and add to the bell peppers. Wash the glove, take it off and hang it to dry.

➤ Heat the ghee in a pot and sauté the onion in it. Add the poultry and fry. Add the curry paste and tomato paste, stir and fry briefly. Now add the pepper and zucchini cubes and fry a little, too. Then deglaze with coconut milk and the vegetable stock and bring to the boil while stirring. Season with a little salt and black pepper. Let everything simmer gently for 5 minutes.

➤ Cut the mango into cubes. At the end, stir in the mango cubes and let them warm up. Season the food with salt and serve warm.

Red Lentil Chard Curry

#ONEPOT #VEGETARIAN #GLUTENFREE

salt
red or yellow chard (9 oz.)
1 medium-sized **onion**
1 **clove of garlic**
1 tablespoon fresh **ginger**
2 tablespoons **butter**
1 teaspoon **cumin powder**
½ teaspoon **turmeric powder**
1 ¼ cups **red lentils** (9 oz.)
1 pack **coconut milk** (14 fl. oz.)
1 ⅔ cups **vegetable stock** (14 fl. oz.)
2 tablespoons **lemon juice**

➤ Bring a pot of lightly salted water to the boil. Wash the chard. Cut the stems and leaves in bite-sized pieces. Blanch the chard pieces in simmering water for 2 minutes and then pour them into a colander.

➤ In the meantime, peel and dice the onions, garlic and ginger. Heat the butter in the used pot. Fry the onions, garlic and ginger in it until translucent. Add cumin and turmeric and fry briefly. Add the lentils, coconut milk and stock. Season with salt and cook everything over medium heat for about 10 minutes. Stir occasionally.

➤ Add the blanched chard to the curry and simmer for another 5 minutes over a low heat. Before serving, season the curry with salt and lemon juice.

Red Lentil and Sweet Potato Curry

#ONEPOT #VEGAN

1 medium **onion**
1 **clove of garlic**
1 **red pointed pepper** (alternatively red bell pepper)
1 medium **sweet potato** (approx. 300 g)
2 tablespoons **olive oil**
2 tablespoons **tomato paste**
1 teaspoon **curry powder**
1 teaspoon **turmeric powder**
½ teaspoon **garam masala**
salt and **black pepper**
10 tablespoons **red lentils** (4.5 oz.)
1 pack **coconut milk** (14 fl. oz.)
⅔ cup **vegetable stock** (5 fl. oz.)

➤ Peel and finely dice the onion and garlic. Wash the peppers and cut them into small cubes. Peel and dice the sweet potatoes in bite-sized pieces.

➤ Heat the olive oil in a pot and sauté the onions until translucent. Add the garlic, fry briefly, and then add the sweet potatoes and peppers to the pot. Add the tomato paste, the spices, as well as salt and black pepper, fry briefly, then add the lentils.

➤ Now pour coconut milk and vegetable stock in the pot and let it simmer for about 25 minutes over low heat. Stir occasionally.

Spicy Beef with Green Beans and Rice

#FAST #MEAT #GLUTENFREE

1 cup of **parboiled long grain rice** (7 oz.)
1 ⅔ cups **water** (14 fl. oz.)
salt
beef sirloin (7 oz., alternatively e.g. flank steak)
1 glass **green beans** (6.3 oz. drained weight)
1 tablespoon **ginger**
3 tablespoons **peanut oil** (alternatively light sesame oil)
1 tablespoon **red curry paste**
3 tablespoons **soy sauce**
¼ teaspoon **black pepper**
1 pinch **sugar**

➤ Bring rice with a little bit of salt to the boil with twice the amount of water. Then simmer the rice on low heat with the lid on, until all the water has been absorbed by the rice.

➤ In the meantime, wash the beef, pat dry and cut into 3 mm thin bite-sized strips. Drain the beans. Finely chop the ginger.

➤ Heat the oil in a second pot and briefly sear the beef, but do not fry it through if possible. Then reduce the heat, stir in the beans, ginger, curry paste, soy sauce, pepper and sugar. Stew for another minute, then place on the plate with the rice and serve.

Thai Soup with Noodles and Chicken

#FAST #ONEPOT #MEAT #GLUTENFREE

1 tablespoon light **sesame oil**
1 **chili pepper** (alternatively curry paste)
1 small **onion**
1 pack **coconut milk** (14 fl. oz.)
2 cups **chicken stock** (17 fl. oz.)
chopped chicken (9 oz., alternatively chicken mince or shrimp)
1 pack **spinach leaves** (7 oz., fresh or frozen, alternatively Brokkoli)
½ pack **glass noodles** (3.5 oz.)
salt and **black pepper**
Soy sauce

➤ Prepare a pot. Put the sesame oil in the pot, but do not heat it yet. Put on a disposable glove. Halve the chili pepper, remove the core, cut into narrow half rings and place in the pot. Finely dice the onion and add to the pot. Wash the glove, take it off and hang it up to dry.

➤ Sauté the chili pepper and onion in a pot. Now add coconut milk and stock and bring to the boil briefly. Now add the meat and simmer for 10 minutes.

➤ Then put the spinach leaves and glass noodles in the pot and simmer for another 5 minutes until the glass noodles and spinach are cooked. Season with a bit of salt and pepper. Serve with soy sauce.

Hearty Salads and Cold dishes

<< 21 savory & nourishing recipes >>

Asian Salad with Peanut Dressing

#VEGETARIAN #GLUTENFREE

2 tablespoons **peanut butter** with peanut pieces (sugar-free)

2 tablespoons **white balsamic vinegar**

3 tablespoons **peanut oil**

1 tablespoon **soy sauce**

3 tablespoons **honey**

1 teaspoon **salt**

¼ teaspoon **chili powder**

1 **lime**

2 tablespoons **coriander greens** (optional)

1 bag or can of **soybeans / edamame** (5 oz., ready to eat)

½ **Chinese cabbage**

1 tablespoon fresh **ginger**

2 medium-sized **carrots**

½ **cucumber**

➤ For the dressing, put peanut butter, vinegar, peanut oil, soy sauce, honey, salt and chili in a glass. Squeeze the lime and add the juice. Chop the coriander greens and add them as well. Mix the dressing thoroughly with a small whisk or fork, and refrigerate until ready to serve.

➤ Drain the soybeans. Cut the Chinese cabbage into fine, bite-sized strips. Peel the ginger and chop it finely. Cut the carrots into thin, 3 cm long sticks. Cut the cucumber into thin quarters.

➤ Put the edamame, Chinese cabbage, carrot, cucumber and ginger in two large bowls and mix it together. Add the dressing just before serving so that everything stays crispy.

ⓘ The rest of the Chinese cabbage tastes good as a side salad with orange fillets.

Bread with Avocado and Tuna

#FAST #FISH

canned **tuna fillet** in its own juice (3 oz.)
3 teaspoons of **capers** (0.7 oz.)
¼ pot **crème fraîche** (2 oz.)
salt and **black pepper**
2 ripe **avocados**
2 stalks of **parsley** (optional)
4 **slices of bread**

➤ Pour off the tuna juice. Then put the tuna in a bowl and chop it up with a fork. Drain the capers, roughly chop them, and add them to the bowl with the tuna. Add the crème fraîche, mix everything thoroughly and season with salt and pepper.

➤ Halve and core the avocados. Remove the pulp from the skin with a tablespoon. Cut the avocados into wedges and place on slices of bread.

➤ Rinse the parsley, shake it dry and chop the leaves. Finally, put the tuna cream on top and sprinkle with parsley.

Bread Salad with Mozzarella

#FAST #VEGETARIAN

dry baguette from the previous day (7 oz., alternatively dry pretzel)
3 cups fresh diced **tomatoes** (21 oz.)
1 cup **yellow cherry tomatoes** (5 oz., alternatively red cherry tomatoes)
1 pack **mozzarella** (4,4 oz.)
1 handful fresh **basil leaves**
10 tablespoons **olive oil**
6 tablespoons **white balsamic vinegar**
salt and **black pepper**

➤ Cut the baguette into bite-sized pieces and put them into two bowls.

➤ Wash all the tomatoes, cut them into small pieces and add them. Cut the mozzarella into small cubes and add it. Wash the basil, shake dry, roughly chop and add it.

➤ Put oil, vinegar, salt and pepper in each bowl and mix the salad well. Let it stand for a few minutes and mix again.

Mushroom and Tuna Salad

#FISH #LOWCARB

6 cups fresh **mushrooms** (17.6 oz., alternatively frozen)
2 cans **tuna** in olive oil (alternatively in its own juice)
½ **lemon**
2 dashes **Tabasco**
2 tablespoons **soy sauce**
salt and **black pepper**
1 handful **parsley leaf**

➤ Cut the fresh mushrooms into slices and fry the fresh or frozen mushrooms in the tuna oil. Alternatively, fry in olive oil. Squeeze the lemon.

➤ Divide the tuna in two bowls and chop up with a fork. Add the mushrooms as soon as they are cooked, and the liquid has evaporated.

➤ Season with lemon juice, Tabasco, soy sauce, salt and black pepper. Chop the parsley and pour over it. Mix the lettuce in both bowls and let it stand for a few minutes.

Cottage Cheese Salad

#FAST #VEGETARIAN #GLUTENFREE

2 tablespoons **pine nuts** (alternatively cedar nuts)
1 cup **cherry tomatoes** (5,4 oz.)
2 tablespoons **black olives** (0.7 oz., seedless, e.g. Kalamon or Kalamata)
Some fresh **basil leaves**
1 pack **cottage cheese** (7 oz.)
salt and **black pepper**
½ **lemon**

➤ Put the nuts in a pan and roast them without oil. Wash tomatoes and cut in half. Cut the olives into rings.

➤ Cut the basil into strips. If necessary, squeeze half of a lemon.

➤ Put the cottage cheese in two bowls. Season with salt, black pepper and lemon juice. Add tomatoes and olives. Sprinkle with pine nuts and basil.

Greek Tomato Salad with Feta

#FAST #VEGETARIAN #GLUTENFREE

4 medium-sized **tomatoes** (14 oz.)
10 **black olives** (seedless, e.g. Kalamon or Kalamata)
feta from sheep's milk (5 oz.)
3 tablespoons **olive oil**
2 tablespoons **white balsamic vinegar**
2 tablespoons **water**
1 teaspoon **medium hot mustard**
1 teaspoon **honey**
salt and **black pepper**

➤ Cut the tomatoes into 1 cm cubes and put them in two bowls. Halve the olives lengthways, cut into small strips and place in the bowls. Cut the feta into small cubes and add.

➤ Mix olive oil, vinegar, water, mustard, honey, salt and pepper to make a salad dressing. Divide the sauce between the two bowls, stir everything briefly and let it stand for a few minutes at room temperature.

Cheese Salad

#MEAT #GLUTENFREE

1 block **cheese** (9 oz., medium-aged Gouda or mountain cheese)
3 **pickled gherkins**
1 **apple**
⅔ cup sliced **ham** (3.5 oz.)
3 tablespoons **liquid from the pickled gherkins jar**
2 tablespoon **natural yogurt**
3 tablespoon **crème fraîche**
1 teaspoon **honey**
1 teaspoon **medium hot mustard**
salt and **black pepper**
1 handful **parsley** (optional)

➤ Coarsely grate the cheese. Dice the pickles, apple and ham. Divide the ingredients between 2 bowls and mix.

➤ Mix the liquid from the pickled gherkins jar, natural yogurt, crème fraîche, honey, mustard, salt and pepper in a separate bowl. Divide the sauce between the two bowls and mix in.

➤ Finely chop the parsley and sprinkle over the salads just before serving.

Smoked Tofu Salad with Chickpeas

#FAST #VEGAN #GLUTENFREE

1 bag or can of **soybeans / edamame** (5 oz., ready to eat)
1 glass **chickpeas** (8 oz. drained weight)
1 package **smoked tofu**
1 glass **green beans** (4.4 oz. drained weight)
1 bunch of **parsley** (optional, alternatively rocket)
½ **lemon**
6 tablespoons **olive oil**
salt and **black pepper**

➤ Drain the soybeans and divide them into two bowls. Wash the chickpeas and add them. Cut the tofu into small cubes and divide.

➤ Drain and add the green beans. Finely chop the parsley and divide. Squeeze the lemon.

➤ Carefully stir the salad in both bowls so that the avocado and beans do not disintegrate and season with oil, lemon juice, salt and pepper.

ⓘ Tofu from the refrigerated shelf tastes "fresher" than tofu that is stored at room temperature.

Crunchy Broccoli Salad

#VEGETARIAN #GLUTENFREE

1 fresh **broccoli** (14 oz.)
1 **red pointed pepper** (alternatively red bell pepper)
1 **apple**
6 tablespoons **olive oil**
3 tablespoons **white balsamic vinegar**
1 tablespoon **mustard**
1 teaspoon **honey**
2 teaspoons **salt**
½ teaspoon **black pepper**

➤ Use the broccoli florets and the soft part of the stalk. Cut the broccoli very small with the multi-chopper and divide it into two bowls.

➤ First cut the pointed pepper and the apple into large pieces. Then cut these very small in the multi-chopper and put them in the two bowls.

➤ Mix oil, vinegar, mustard, honey, salt and black pepper to make a salad dressing. Divide the salad dressing between the two bowls, stir well and eat the salad straight away.

ⓘ Fresh broccoli can be eaten raw without hesitation.

Kohlrabi Salad with Feta and Cranberries

#VEGETARIAN #GLUTENFREE

2 small **kohlrabi**
2 small **apples**
2 handful **rocket** (1.8 oz.)
4 tablespoons **walnuts** (1.8 oz.)
1 **lemon**
6 tablespoons **olive oil**
4 tablespoons **white balsamic vinegar**
salt and **black pepper**
feta from sheep's milk (3,5 oz.)
4 tablespoons **dried cranberries**

➤ Peel the kohlrabi, cut it into 2-3 cm pieces and then into small pieces with the multi-chopper. Wash the apples, remove the core, cut into pieces without peeling and also chop in the multi-chopper.

➤ Divide the kohlrabi and apples into two bowls. Roughly chop the rocket and walnut kernels with the knife and place in the bowls. Squeeze the lemon.

➤ Add the lemon juice, olive oil, vinegar, salt and pepper and mix well. Crumble the feta by hand and pour over the salads. Scatter cranberries on top and serve.

ⓘ If you don't have a multi-chopper at hand, you can grate the kohlrabi coarsely.

Lentil Salad with Carrots and Apple

#FAST #VEGAN

1 glas of cooked **brown lentils**
2 medium-sized **carrots** (5 oz.)
1 large **apple**
4 tablespoons **soy sauce**
2 tablespoons **white balsamic vinegar**
6 tablespoons **olive oil**
2 tablespoons **sunflower seeds**
little **salt** and **black pepper**

➤ Roast the sunflower seeds without oil in a pan until lightly browned.

➤ Drain the lentils and divide them into two bowls. Cut each carrot into 2-3 cm pieces and cut into small pieces one after the other with the multi-chopper. Wash the apples, remove the core, cut into pieces without peeling and also chop in the multi-chopper. Divide the carrots and apple between the two bowls.

➤ Put half each of the soy sauce, vinegar, olive oil, salt and pepper in a bowl and mix everything together well. Pour the sunflower seeds on top and serve.

ⓘ If you don't have a multi-chopper at hand, you can cut the carrots into thin strips with a knife and then dice them finely. The apple is also diced with a knife without peeling.

Lentil and Tomato Salad

#FAST #VEGAN #GLUTENFREE

1 small **zucchini**
1 **clove of garlic**
6 tablespoons **olive oil**
10 **soft tomatoes** (2.8 oz., alternatively pickled or fresh tomatoes)
5 stems **basil**
1 glass of **lentils** (8 oz. drained weight)
3 tablespoons **white balsamic vinegar**
salt and **black pepper**

➤ Put on a disposable glove. Dice zucchini and garlic and sauté in a pot with 2 tablespoons of olive oil over low heat. Wash the glove, take it off and hang it to dry.

➤ Cut the soft tomatoes into small cubes and finely chop the basil. Drain the lentils. Turn off the stove.

➤ Put the tomatoes, basil, lentils, vinegar and the rest of the oil in the pot. Season only with a little salt and a little pepper, as the soft tomatoes already taste salty. Divide between two bowls and serve lukewarm.

Mackerel Rillette With Bread

#FAST #FISH

1 can **mackerel fillet** (5 oz.)
1 pack all natural **cream cheese** (5 oz.)
2 **capers**
½ **lemon**
4 **slices of bread**

➤ Pour off the liquid from the mackerel fillet can, put the fish in a bowl, and use forks to coarsely shred the fillet.

➤ Chop the capers. Squeeze the lemon.

➤ Add the cream cheese, chopped capers and lemon juice to taste and mix well with a fork. Serve the spread with bread.

Mediterranean Broccoli Salad

#FAST #VEGETARIAN #LOWCARB #GLUTENFREE

1 fresh **broccoli** (14 oz.)
salt
water
8 **soft tomatoes** (2.5 oz.)
1 cup **cherry tomatoes** (5 oz.)
salt and **black pepper**
light balsamic vinegar
olive oil
½ bunch flat-leaf **parsley**
feta from sheep's milk (5 oz.)

➤ Clean the broccoli, cut into florets, and cook in salted water for about five minutes. It should be al dente when it's poured off.

➤ Cut the soft tomatoes into small pieces, halve the cherry tomatoes and divide both with the cooled broccoli in two bowls. Mix salt and black pepper with the vinegar, add the olive oil. Cut the parsley into small pieces.

➤ Mix the dressing and the parsley with the vegetables, cut the feta into cubes and sprinkle on top.

Mediterranean Tortellini Salad

1 pack **tortellini** (9 oz., with cheese filling from the cooling shelf)
salt
2 tablespoons **pine nuts** (alternatively cedar nuts)
6 **soft tomatoes** (1.8 oz.)
2 handfuls of **lamb's lettuce** (0.9 oz., alternatively rocket)
12 **cherry tomatoes** (3.5 oz.)
1,4 oz. **Parmesan** (in one piece or coarsely grated)
6 tablespoons **olive oil**
3 tablespoons **white balsamic vinegar**
salt and **black pepper**
1 teaspoon **honey**

➤ Cook the tortellini in salted water according to the instructions on the packet. Roast the nuts in a pan without oil until they brown. Stir occasionally. Cut the soft tomatoes into small strips. Wash the lamb's lettuce. Halve the cherry tomatoes. Coarsely grate the Parmesan, if necessary.

➤ Rinse the tortellini in cold water, drain them well and return them to the pot with 1 tablespoon of olive oil and mix them together so that they do not stick together. Put in the soft tomatoes, cherry tomatoes and nuts and mix. Cut the lamb's lettuce into bite-sized pieces and add.

➤ Mix the remaining olive oil, vinegar, salt, pepper and honey into a vinaigrette and add it to the salad. Divide the salad between two bowls, sprinkle with the Parmesan and serve.

Beetroot Chickpea Salad

#FAST #VEGETARIAN #GLUTENFREE

1 glass **chickpeas** (8 oz. drained weight)
1 glas **beetroot** (8 oz. drained weight)
feta from sheep's milk (5 oz.)
1 handful fresh **basil leaves**
½ **lemon**
3 tablespoons **olive oil**
salt and **black pepper**

➤ Drain the chickpeas in a colander, wash them and divide them into two bowls. If necessary cut the beetroot into bite-sized pieces and add to the chickpeas.

➤ Dice the feta cheese, roughly chop the basil and squeeze the lemon. Divide all ingredients between the two bowls and mix. Season to taste with lemon juice, olive oil, salt and black pepper.

ⓘ If you want to pre-cook the beetroot yourself, it is best to buy the fresh tubers from late summer to March. The smaller they are, the more delicate they taste. So that as little of the healthy ingredients as possible are lost during preparation, you should cook the beetroot with the peel. Wash and brush them gently without damaging the skin. Cook the beetroot in water (without salt) for at least 30 minutes. It's done when you can prick it easily with a knife. After cooking, you can rub the skin of the beetroot with a knife and cut the tuber into pieces. If there is a splash of beetroot juice anywhere, you can remove it with hot water and citric acid. If you eat large amounts of beetroot, the urine or stool can turn reddish for a short time.

Beetroot Salad with Gouda and Rocket

#FAST #VEGETARIAN #GLUTENFREE

1 glas **beetroot** (8 oz. drained weight)
1 handful of young **rocket** (alternatively pickled gherkins)
1 **apple**
piece of **Gouda** (3.5 oz., medium-aged)
1 handful **walnuts**
1 teaspoon **medium-hot mustard**
6 tablespoons **olive oil**
4 tablespoons **white balsamic vinegar**
salt and **black pepper**

➤ If necessary cut the beetroot into small cubes and divide between two bowls.

➤ Cut the rocket into small pieces, cut the apple and Gouda cheese into very small pieces, chop the walnuts and divide everything into the bowls.

➤ Mix the salad dressing made of mustard, olive oil, vinegar, salt and pepper in a glass with a whisk. Divide the salad dressing between the bowls and stir the two salads before serving.

ⓘ You can also pre-cook the beetroot yourself. Instructions for this can be found at the end of the recipe for the "Beetroot Chickpea Salad".

White Bean Tomato Tuna Salad

#FAST #FISH #GLUTENFREE

1 glass of **small white beans** (e.g. canellini, 8.5 oz. drained weight)
2 medium-sized **tomatoes** (7 oz.)
1 can **tuna** in olive oil (6.5 oz.)
1 handful **parsley flat leaf**
½ **lemon**
salt and **black pepper**

➤ Drain the beans, rinse under cold water and place in two bowls. Wash the tomatoes, remove the stalks, cut into 1 cm pieces and divide between the two bowls.

➤ Divide the tuna between the two salad bowls and use a fork or spoon to cut into pieces. Rinse the parsley, shake dry, roughly chop and place in the bowls.

➤ Squeeze half a lemon and distribute the juice between the bowls. Season with salt and black pepper. Mix the salad ingredients together.

Tuna Salad with Cucumber, Corn and Pepper

#FAST #FISH #GLUTENFREE

1 can **tuna** in olive oil (6.5 oz.)
1 **red pointed pepper** (alternatively red bell pepper)
½ **cucumber**
1 glass of **corn** (10.5 oz.)
1 teaspoon medium-hot **mustard**
6 tablespoons **white balsamic vinegar**

➤ Put the olive oil of the tuna in a glass. Put the tuna in two bowls and chop with a fork.

➤ Wash and clean the pointed peppers and cucumber, cut them into cubes and divide the pieces between the two bowls. Drain the corn, divide between the two bowls and mix in.

➤ Add the mustard and vinegar to the olive oil glass. Mix the dressing with a small whisk and pour over the salad.

Warm Pasta Salad with Tomatoes and Feta

#FAST #VEGETARIAN

3 cups **fusilli** (10.5 oz.)
5 tablespoons **pine nuts** (2 oz., alternatively cedar nuts)
12 **soft tomatoes** (3.5 oz.)
feta from sheep's milk (3,5 oz.)
1 handful fresh **basil leaves**
olive oil
salt and **black pepper**

➤ Make the pasta al dente according to the instructions on the package. Roast the nuts in a pan without fat.

➤ In the meantime, cut the soft tomatoes into small pieces, dice the feta and cut the basil leaves into small pieces.

➤ Drain the cooked pasta and put everything back in the pot. Now pour some olive oil over it and season with salt and pepper. Put the pasta salad in two bowls and eat it warm.

Watermelon Salad with Feta

#FAST #VEGETARIAN #GLUTENFREE

2 tablespoons **pumpkin seeds**
2 tablespoons **sunflower seeds**
olive oil
salt and **black pepper**
chili powder
½ small **watermelon**
feta from sheep's milk (5 oz.)
1 handful fresh **mint**
2 **limes**

➤ Roast pumpkin seeds and sunflower seeds in a pan with a little olive oil, salt, black pepper and chili powder. Stir until the kernels brown and then remove from the heat.

➤ Peel the watermelon and remove the seeds as much as possible. Cut the watermelon into bite-sized pieces. Chop the mint into strips. Place the watermelon and mint in two bowls. Cut the feta into bite-sized pieces.

➤ Squeeze a lime over each of the bowls. Add a little olive oil, salt and pepper and stir the two bowls. Divide the feta between the two bowls. Scatter the roasted seeds on top and serve.

Side Salads

<< 4 raw vegetable salads for the multi-chopper>>

Fennel Salad

#FAST #VEGAN #GLUTENFREE

1 **fennel** (9 oz.)
2 teaspoons of **lemon juice**
4 tablespoons **olive oil**
2 tablespoons **white balsamic vinegar**
salt and **black pepper**

➤ Wash the fennel, remove the stalk and cut it into pieces approx. 2 cm in size.

➤ Put the first half of the fennel pieces in the multi-chopper. Add a teaspoon of lemon juice to prevent the fennel from browning. Crush the contents thoroughly and pour into a small bowl. Then do the same with the second half. Rinse the multi-chopper with water.

➤ Put half of the olive oil and vinegar in each bowl. Mix the salads and season with salt and black pepper.

Carrot and Apple Salad

1 **apple**
2 **carrots** (7 oz., alternatively celery)
4 tablespoons **olive oil**
2 tablespoons **white balsamic vinegar**
salt and **black pepper**
2 teaspoons **sunflower seeds** (optional)

➤ Wash, core and cut the apple. The peel of the apple and carrots can also be eaten. Wash the carrots and cut off the top ends. Remove green spots as they can taste a bit bitter. Cut the carrots into pieces about 1 cm long.

➤ Put the first half of the apple pieces and the carrot pieces in the multi-chopper. Crush the contents thoroughly and pour into a small bowl. Then do the same with the second half.

➤ Rinse the multi-chopper with water. Add half the olive oil and vinegar to each bowl. Mix the salads and season with salt and pepper. Scatter sunflower seeds on top and serve.

Kohlrabi Salad

#FAST #VEGETARIAN #GLUTENFREE

1 **kohlrabi**
1 tablespoon **olive oil**
1 tablespoon **white balsamic vinegar**
2 teaspoons **honey**
2 tablespoons **natural yogurt**
salt and **black pepper** (alternatively 2 teaspoons vegetable stock paste)

➤ Peel the kohlrabi and cut it into pieces approx. 2 cm in size.

➤ Put the first half of the kohlrabi pieces in the multi-chopper. Crush the contents thoroughly and pour into a small bowl. Then do the same with the second half. Rinse the multi-chopper with water.

➤ Put half of the olive oil, vinegar, honey and yogurt in each bowl. Mix the salads and season with salt and black pepper or, if available, with the vegetable stock paste.

Celery Salad

#FAST #VEGETARIAN #GLUTENFREE

½ **celery tuber** (10.5 oz.)
2 tablespoons **olive oil**
2 tablespoons **white balsamic vinegar**
¼ cup all natural **sour cream** (2 oz., alternatively natural yogurt)
1 pinch sugar
salt and black **pepper** (or 1 teaspoon vegetable stock paste)

➤ Peel celery and cut it into pieces approx. 2 cm in size.

➤ Put the first half of the celery pieces in the multi-chopper. Crush the contents thoroughly and pour into a small bowl. Then do the same with the second half. Rinse the multi-chopper with water.

➤ Whisk olive oil, vinegar, sour cream, sugar, salt and pepper in a glass. Stir the dressing halfway into the salads and season again to taste.

Acknowledgments

This cookbook is self-published. With passion, night shifts and encouragement from friends and family. Despite the amount of work, I really love to write down my knowledge and publish inspiring books on Amazon. Every purchase and every review keeps me going.

 If you enjoyed my cookbook, please write a review on Amazon. I am so excited to read your thoughts. Thank you!

Printed in Great Britain
by Amazon

33980726R00062